WOMEN WHO LED THE WAY

GREAT EXPLORERS AND ADVENTURERS

Dedicated to the United Nations' International Women's Day

Text and illustrations copyright © Mick Manning and Brita Granström 2022

The right of Mick Manning and Brita Granström to be identified as the authors
and illustrators of this work has been asserted by them in accordance with the
Copyright, Designs and Patents Act, 1988 (United Kingdom).

First published in Great Britain in 2022 by
Otter-Barry Books, Little Orchard, Burley Gate, Herefordshire, HR1 3QS.
This paperback edition first published in Great Britain in 2023 by Otter-Barry Books

www.otterbarrybooks.com

A catalogue record for this book is available from the British Library

ISBN 978-1-91565-908-8

Illustrated with watercolour and pencil
www.mickandbrita.com

Printed in China

9 8 7 6 5 4 3 2

WOMEN WHO LED THE WAY

GREAT EXPLORERS AND ADVENTURERS

MICK MANNING AND BRITA GRANSTRÖM

Otter-Barry BOOKS

Contents

Other Great Women Explorers featured...

A Message from Brita Granström

I've loved making this book and choosing some of my heroes as examples of the incredible courage, determination and power of women explorers from all over the world.

For over 1200 years we women have led the way, overcoming not only natural obstacles and dangers but also the view that women should not take part in such activities at all!

From Aud the Deep-Minded to Mae Jemison, from Sacagawea to Barbara Hillary, women have explored and discovered; from the sea bed to outer space and in the fields of science, history, archaeology, ecology and social injustice.

As you meet them, and listen to their own amazing stories of travel and discovery, you will realise that not even the sky is the limit to what we women have achieved and can achieve in the future.

As space-explorer Mae Jemison tells us:

It's your life. Go on and do all you can with it.

Be inspired! Be yourself!
Take up the challenge!

Brita Granström

Aud the Deep-Minded

Mid 9th century, Scotland/Ireland
Early Voyager to Iceland

Another great explorer...

Gudridur Thorbjarnardottir (born 10th century, Iceland), after travelling to live in Greenland, later journeyed with her husband, Thorfinn, to explore Vinland (North America). Their baby, Snorri, was the first European to be born there. But life became too hard and they had to sail back to Greenland.

Aud's Story

I was always thoughtful and strong-willed. My father, Ketil Flatnose, was the Viking ruler of the Hebrides and he married me to a warrior named Olaf the White, the ruler of Dublin. I lived there for many years but when a feud erupted between Olaf and my father, I returned to the Hebrides, taking our red-haired son, Thorsten, with me.

Thorsten the Red became a great warrior. He conquered the north of Scotland and had six beautiful daughters. We settled there until Thorsten was betrayed and killed in battle. With traitors everywhere, it was no longer safe for us…. I thought long and hard: what could a grandmother do? Then I had the answer. I had a ship built in secret, and with a crew of twenty loyal warriors, I captained a voyage of discovery and escape.

We sailed north, over mountainous waves to Iceland, the edge of the known world. We explored that magical place of icy glaciers and fiery volcanoes until we found a good place to live. Then we settled there.

I soon found we were the only Christians. The Icelandic people still worshipped the old gods: Freyr, Thor and Odin. So I set up a Christian cross on a hillside and encouraged others to pray with me. Over time, many joined us on that windy hill, although some still wore Thor's hammer beside their cross! I lived the rest of my life in that beautiful land of ice and fire… and freedom for strong-willed women.

Jeanne Baret's story

Let me tell you what I did for love! In 1765 Philibert Commerson, the man I loved, was invited to be ship's naturalist on a round-the-world expedition under Captain Bougainville. I wasn't allowed to go too, because no women were allowed on sailing ships in those days. But Philibert knew the navy would allow him to take a servant. So we hatched a daring plan… Philibert would hire a young manservant… me!

All went well at first. When we reached the South American coast, Philibert and I went ashore to explore and to collect plant, stone and shell specimens for study. In Brazil we discovered a new plant – which was later named Bougainvillea. Exploring was dangerous work: there were pirates and poisonous snakes and one of our expedition was murdered in Rio de Janeiro! Three years went by and our secret seemed to be safe. But then we landed in Tahiti….

Suddenly I found myself surrounded by islanders laughing and pointing at me! They were shouting out in Tahitian that I was a woman! I had to be rushed back to the ship, but my secret was out. We left the ship after reaching the beautiful island of Mauritius and lived happily there for the rest of Philibert's life.

I returned to France in 1775 – the first woman to have sailed round the world!

Another great explorer…

Laura Dekker (born 1995) is a New Zealand-born Dutch sailor and the youngest person to circumnavigate the globe single-handed. Setting out at only 14 years old, her voyage took two years, in a red ketch called *Guppy*.

Jeanne Baret

1740 -1807, France

First woman to travel round the world

I had to pretend to be a boy!

Caroline Herschel

1750 -1848, Germany/UK

Astronomer who discovered eight comets

It was lonely and often cold work, spending the starlight nights on a grass-plot without another human being nearby.

Another great explorer...

Merieme Chadid (born 1969, Morocco/France) is a leading 21st century astronomer. She has worked on the installation of the *Very Large Telescope* in Chile and, as part of her commitment to setting up an observatory in Antarctica, she became the first Moroccan *and* first French woman to reach the South Pole and the first to plant a Moroccan flag there.

Caroline Herschel's story

As a child, a disease called Typhus slowed my growth as well as damaging the vision in my left eye. But nevertheless I grew up to be a sought-after singer, joining my brother William who was working as a musician in England. However, he and I had another shared interest – the night sky – and that became more important to us even than music.

At first I helped my brother with his studies like a well-trained puppy: cooking, cleaning and writing down his notes while he looked through his telescope. However, as William spent so much time building new telescopes, I also got to star-gaze. Peering through that tiny lens, I found myself far out in space: an explorer of the stars with just the blink of my eye.

In 1782 my brother was appointed court astronomer to King George III and was able to build a powerful reflecting telescope. With this I became very good at discovering comets. When my brother showed my first comet discovery to the Royal Family they gave me loud applause. Over the years I spotted seven more comets (the last without even using a telescope) and I too was paid a salary from the king.

By 1828 The Royal Astronomical Society had awarded me their gold medal and in 1835 I was elected as an Honorary Member! But worth more to me than any gold medals was my telescope and the freedom it gave me to explore the Milky Way and discover not only eight comets but a dwarf elliptical galaxy 2.5 million light years away.... Not bad work for a visually impaired astronomer, let alone a young woman of the 18th century!

There are layers of history beneath our feet!

Another great explorer...

Isabella Bird (1831-1904) was a British explorer and world traveller who, despite being seriously ill with a spinal tumour, explored America in the 1870s. Riding hundreds of miles on horseback, Isabella made friends with a one-eyed desperado named Rocky-Mountain Jim and wrote books and articles. She became the first woman to be elected a Fellow of the Royal Geographical Society.

Lady Hester Lucy Stanhope

1776 -1839, UK

Desert explorer and first archaeologist of the Holy Land

Hester Stanhope's story

I was born into one of the most influential families in England. My uncle, William Pitt the Younger, was a British prime minister and I became his secretary. I was happy for some years but in 1810, after being disappointed in love, I decided to leave England for ever and explore the mysteries of the Middle East.

On my way to Cairo I survived a shipwreck. Needing dry clothes, I chose mannish fashions: purple jackets, embroidered trousers and a sword… much better for travelling; and I travelled in style.

Then, in 1815, I came into possession of something very exciting: a medieval document that I realised was a sort of treasure map showing that three million gold coins were buried under the ruins of a Syrian mosque. I persuaded the authorities to let me explore the ruins. But I was no mere treasure hunter. I carefully studied every layer of history below my feet: I found there had been a pagan temple, then a church and finally a beautiful mosque. Although I never found the coins, there, among the ruins of Ashkelon, I became the first archaeologist to use an ancient text as a source, and the first to carry out a modern analysis of the site I was exploring.

Hester Stanhope rode an Arab stallion and needed 22 camels to carry her baggage! The first European woman to cross the Syrian desert, she was known as *Queen of the Desert*.

13

Sacagawea

1788 - 1812, Shoshone Nation, USA

Guide and interpreter on the Lewis and Clark expedition

Sacagawea's story

My name means Boat Pusher and I was born into the mighty Shoshone nation. When I was a girl of only 12, I was captured by an enemy tribe and sold to a fur trapper, who made me his wife. Then, when I was about 16, some soldiers hired my husband to guide them upriver.

Captains Meriwether Lewis and William Clark were the leaders of the Corps of Discovery, mapping a route across my beloved native lands, and they asked me to go with them. My baby boy, Jean Baptiste, came too as the youngest member of the expedition and our new friends nicknamed him Little Pompy! I soon proved my value: a canoe turned over and I rescued their precious log books and other paperwork from a watery grave. Lewis and Clark named the river after me – the Sacagawea River. I showed them how to live off the land and we had many adventures: fording rivers, climbing mountains, even being attacked by grizzly bears….

When we needed to buy horses to cross the Rocky Mountains, I was asked to go and meet a Shoshone chief. I found he was my long-lost brother, One Who Never Walks. I wept and danced with joy and he was so delighted he gave us the horses. A hard crossing we had of those mountains! We were so short of food we were forced to eat tallow candles (made with animal fat) to survive. Once on the other side I used my survival skills, gathering and cooking nourishing plants to regain our strength.

Our expedition took several years and became famous. Afterwards my husband and I settled in St Louis, Missouri. Pompy grew up to become a friend of European royals, a magistrate and a gold prospector. Me? Well, my face is on a special American coin and my name is in the history books.

Another great explorer...

Marie Aioe Dorion Venier Toupin (1786-1850, Iowa Nation) was known as Walks Far Woman and was the only female member of an overland expedition to the Pacific Northwest. When her husband was killed and scalped by Bannock warriors, she made her way to safety with her two young children, surviving for 50 days by living off the land.

Mary Anning

1799 –1847, UK

Pioneering fossil explorer

Many of Mary's discoveries, including this magnificent Plesiosaur, can be seen today in the Natural History Museum in London.

In 2010, almost 200 years after her death, Mary was listed by The Royal Society as one of the top ten women to influence the development of science.

Mary Anning's story

I was born in Lyme Regis on the Dorset coast. My father was a poor cabinet-maker who also sold fossils collected from the seashore to make extra money, and I helped him. When my father died in 1810, my mother encouraged me to continue fossil hunting, to help put food on the table….

In 1811 my brother discovered something very exciting – a huge fossil skull embedded in the cliff. It was a great discovery, yet I felt there was more to come. I searched for weeks and at last found the rest of its skeleton. At first the fossil was thought to be an ancient crocodile. But when I found a complete specimen that was over 19 feet (6 metres) long, scientists realised this was a new sort of prehistoric sea reptile. They named it *Ichthyosaur*. Then, in 1823, I found a huge fossil creature with such a long neck that at first some experts thought I had made a fake. Scientists named this one *Plesiosaurus*.

By now scientists were travelling from as far as New York to come fossil-hunting with me. In 1828 I discovered the tangled bones of what turned out to be a flying reptile, a *Pterosaur*, that caused a public sensation when it was displayed in London.

Despite finding hundreds of fossils, studying anatomy and carefully drawing my finds in letters to my scientific customers, I was rarely even mentioned in those men's essays and lectures. The Geological Society, to which they belonged, refused even to allow me to attend their lectures on *my* fossil finds!

From six years old, Mary was her father's fossil-collecting assistant. Fossils are prehistoric creatures or plants whose remains became buried in mud, sand or silt. Over millions of years this becomes rock.

Mary went on to dodge high tides and survive cliff landslides, searching on her own or with her friend Elizabeth Philpott, to bring the world her discoveries. Yet she was never given the credit she deserved in her lifetime.

Harriet 'Moses' Tubman

1818 -1902, USA

Escaped slave, army scout and political activist

Harriet Tubman's story

I was born a slave on a plantation in Maryland, America, and I suffered extreme cruelty. But I escaped by using the 'underground railroad', a cross-country network of people opposed to slavery.

I trusted in the Lord to keep me safe from the slave-catchers, who pursued me with their fierce dogs. I travelled by night, following the North Star as I passed from safe house to safe house. Finally I reached Philadelphia, where slavery had been abolished. *'When I found I had crossed that line, I looked at my hands to see if I was the same person. There was such a glory over everything, and I felt like I was in Heaven.'*

But I felt so sorry for those I had left behind that I soon went back to free others. Over 11 years I helped more than 70 enslaved people to escape and every time I praised God. I felt like Moses bringing my people to the Promised Land — and that became my codename.

In 1861 the American Civil War began, between the Union states and the Confederate states, who supported slavery. I led a band of army scouts. In the Combahee River raid of 1863 I became the first woman to lead an armed attack. I led the troops upriver in three steamboats to destroy slave plantations. We freed over 750 slaves that day.

> Don't ever stop, Keep going. If you want a taste of freedom, keep going!

Another great explorer...

Mary Seacole (1805-1881, Jamaica/UK) risked everything to help nurse the wounded during the Crimean War. Travelling to the Crimea on her own initiative and lacking any official funding, Mary built a 'British Hotel' for her soldiers out of driftwood and salvaged scrap metal. In 2004 she was voted the greatest Black Briton.

Nellie Bly's story

When I was a child, my name was Elizabeth Cochran. My father was a mill owner, but he died when I was still at school. After that my mother and I moved to Pittsburgh.

One day I read an article in the local paper that said girls were only good for having babies and being housewives! *What?* I wrote an angry letter to the editor, using the pseudonym 'lonely orphan girl', and he commissioned an article from me. Soon I had a full-time job as a journalist and I began to use the pen-name Nellie Bly.

In New York I persuaded the *New York World* newspaper to let me go undercover to investigate rumours of cruelty to patients at the Women's Lunatic Asylum on Blackwell Island. But first, to get there I had to be certified as insane. So I went to a boarding house and shouted and screamed until the police took me away. I was locked in the Lunatic Asylum and found that the rumours of mistreatment were true – it was a terrible place run by bullies!

After ten days the newspaper got me out! I wrote a blistering article revealing the truth, which forced the hospital to change its ways. *But what to do next?*

Well, having enjoyed Jules Verne's book, *Around the World in Eighty Days*, I decided to turn fiction into fact, reporting back to my readers about it every step of the way! I took a steamer to England and from there I travelled east by boat and railroad... I travelled through France, the Suez Canal, Ceylon, Singapore and China, sending reports back to my newspaper by telegraph. Travelling alone, I circumnavigated the globe, finally arriving back in the USA after a journey of seventy-two days. I had made a world record – eight days faster than Jules Verne's fictional hero Phileas Fogg!

The police took Nellie away to the Women's Lunatic Asylum on Blackwell Island. Exactly as she had planned.

Nellie Bly

1864 -1922, USA

America's first female undercover journalist and record-breaking round-the-world traveller

I mustn't miss my connection!

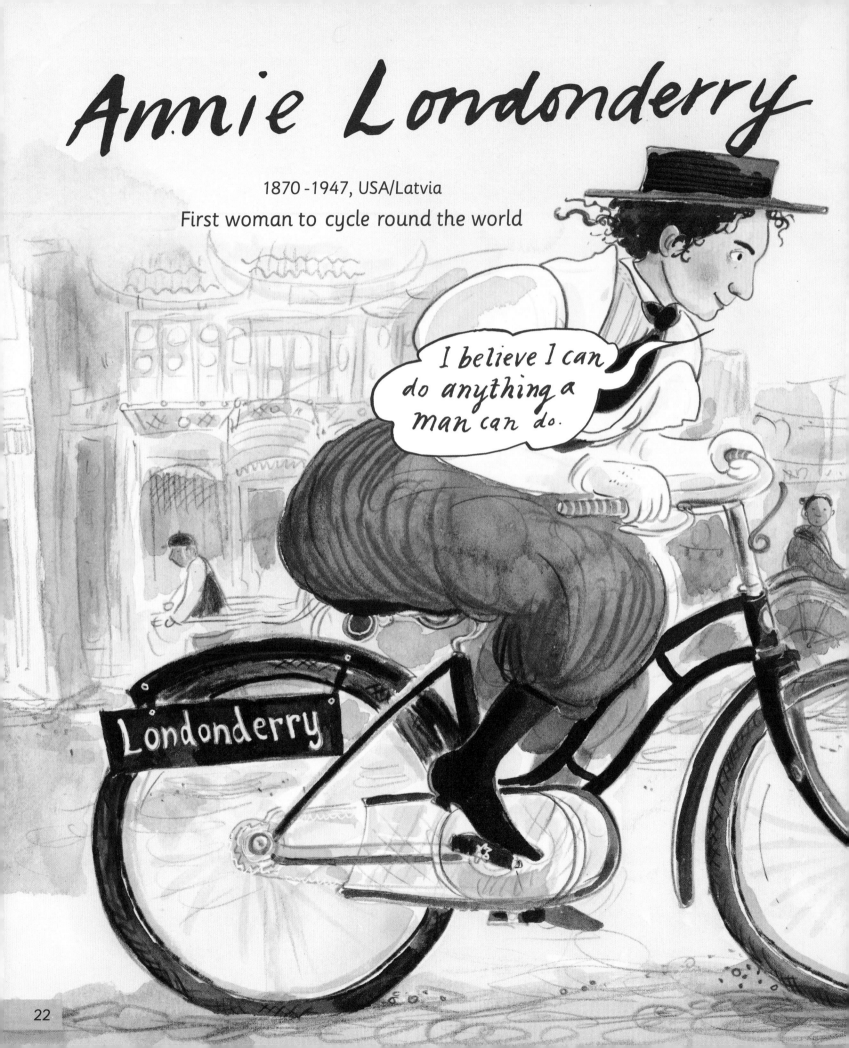

Annie Londonderry's story

I came to the USA from Latvia aged only five, and my family was very poor. I was an orphan by the time I was 17. But I had big dreams, and I planned a world-wide adventure inspired by the new craze for bicycles.

First I needed funding, so I told my first fib: that two rich gentlemen had offered me a prize of 10,000 dollars to be the first woman to cycle around the world! That got me in the papers and my publicity stunt persuaded Londonderry Spring Water to fund me. In return I called myself Annie Londonderry and carried their name on my back wheel.

My bike was heavy and hard to pedal in thick skirts. With winter coming, I was almost ready to give up. But then Sterling Cycle Works sponsored me with a beautiful lightweight bike and from then on I pedalled in my bloomers!

In France my imagination took over. I made up all sorts of stories about myself for the press: I was a wealthy heiress, an inventor/medical student/US senator's niece…. I realised I could travel a lot easier and faster if I took trains and steamships between my bike rides through Egypt, Jerusalem, Yemen, Ceylon, Vietnam and China.

By March 1895 I was sailing back to the USA. There I gave lectures to huge audiences and I didn't hold back! I told them I had hunted tigers in India, been in a Japanese prison, and even sold copies of a staged photo of myself being robbed by outlaws.

But it wasn't all fibs. When invited to tell about my adventures in the *New Woman* magazine, I wrote: *'I believe I can do anything that any man can do.'*

Now, that is the truth!

In France the authorities confiscated Annie's bike until her passport had been cleared. But it gave her time to make up more stories.

Ester Blenda Nordström

1891-1948, Sweden

First Swedish investigative journalist and undercover reporter

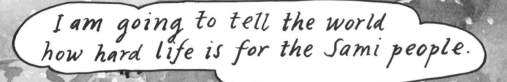

Ester Nordström's story

My name is Ester, and from a young age I shocked my well-to-do parents by being a 'tomboy'. I loved to do the things boys did. I grew up to become what is now known as an investigative journalist, writing under my nickname 'The Boy' and later as 'Bansai'.

In 1914, when I was only 23, I went undercover for a national newspaper to live and work as a poorly paid Swedish farm servant. I found the days to be long and hard, but also full of comradeship. I was well-liked by the farmer and his family. They were heartbroken when I admitted I had been sending reports to the newspaper. My articles made me famous, but I knew I had betrayed that family's trust.

My next adventure as a journalist was to drive across Sweden on a huge motorcycle. Then I went to live and work as a teacher for a year in Lapland with the nomadic Sami people.

In 1922 I travelled on a steamship to New York with poor Swedish emigrants hoping to find a better life in America. I worked as a waitress and kitchen drudge, and later I hitchhiked alone across the USA. I found poverty and courage but also many shattered dreams. My groundbreaking reports both shocked and informed my readers – and changed Swedish journalism for ever.

For a month Ester worked as a farm servant: cooking, cleaning, milking, baking and doing farm work with the other servants.

In Lapland she taught Sami children and wrote about the hard life of the Sami reindeer farmers.

She travelled on a steamer to New York and reported back to the newspapers about the poorest Swedes, who were desperate for a new life in America.

25

Bessie Coleman's story

I was born to a poor family of cotton share-croppers in Texas. My daddy was of the Cherokee nation and my mommy was an African-American. I studied at a 'blacks only' school, forbidden to mix with white children. To cut a long story short, when I was old enough, I moved to Chicago to live with my brothers and got a job as a manicurist. That's where war-pilots' flying tales inspired me to want to be a flyer.

But flight schools in the USA didn't admit women or African-Americans back then. So, after a course in speaking French, I worked hard to raise money to go to Europe for flight lessons. In 1921 I became the first black woman to get a pilot's licence. I wanted to earn my living as a 'Barnstormer' – a dare-devil stunt flyer! Back in the USA my first major event was at an airshow held to honour the all-black 369th infantry regiment. I showed those boys what a girl could do! I gave them figure-of-eight loops, upside-down flying and I zoomed so near the ground it was known as 'daisy cutting'.

I became known as Queen Bess. Once I crashed and broke a leg and three ribs – but I never gave up, and I always refused to fly in events that banned African Americans.

I just loved to fly – and sometimes it felt like the sky was the only place free from racial prejudice.

Bessie was a fearless adventurer, often hanging from the wings in her barnstorming circus performances. She led the way for women – and especially black women – to become pilots and ultimately astronauts.

Amelia Earhart

1897–1937, USA

First female pilot to fly across the Atlantic Ocean

Amelia Earhart's story

As a child, I played all sorts of crazy games with my sister, imagining we were flying! In 1920 I was taken up in an aeroplane and from that moment I just knew I had to be a flyer. I was trained by a female pilot named Anita Snook, and six months later I bought my own beautiful little yellow biplane (a plane with two sets of wings, one above the other). I called her *Canary*. In 1922, my brave yellow bird flew me to an altitude of 14,000 feet (4,300 metres), making me the world record holder for female pilots.

In 1932 I flew solo from Canada to Ireland, crossing the Atlantic Ocean in just under 15 hours. I faced icy winds and mechanical problems on my lonely voyage but eventually, with a gentle bump, my lovely red Lockheed Vega landed safely in a field in Northern Ireland.

Flying was my life, and after many other adventures I was determined to be the first woman to fly round the world. I set off in 1937, taking another pilot, Fred Noonan, as my navigator. We flew a beautiful silver Lockheed Electra. At first things went well, but over the Pacific Ocean our fuel ran out. We were never seen again, but my fame lives on as a brave pioneer of flight.

When she was a child, Amelia spent her days exploring and climbing trees with her sister, Grace. They even built a dangerous ramp on top of the garden shed and whizzed off it on a sledge. Luckily for Amelia, she only tore her clothes and bruised her hip – but it was her first 'flight'!

...what do dreams know of boundaries?

Another great explorer...

Australia's Angel of the Outback

Nancy Bird Walton (1915 - 2009) gained her pilot's licence in 1933. Due to her flights as an air ambulance pilot and her work ferrying nurses to remote areas of the Australian outback, she soon became known as the 'Angel of the Outback'. Nancy was also the first Australian woman to fly passenger planes and during the Second World War (1939 - 1945) she trained other women to be pilots. In 1997 she was declared a 'National Treasure', keeping her flying licence until the age of 90.

Lee Miller

1907-1977, USA

Pioneering photojournalist

Being a good photojournalist is like sitting on a branch and sawing it off behind you!

Lee Miller's story

I was born and brought up in New York, but in 1925 I went to stage school in Paris, then art school in Manhattan. I became the most popular fashion model in New York, photographed by the leading fashion photographers of the day. These were all men....

Why, I wondered, couldn't I earn a dime as a woman photographer? So I learned from the best, the artist and photographer Man Ray, and through him I met and photographed Pablo Picasso and Jean Cocteau.

Everything changed with the outbreak of the Second World War. I was living in London, where Vogue magazine asked me to be their official war photographer. I explored the ruins of bombed-out streets, photographing the devastation to show American people what was being done to Europe by Adolf Hitler and his Nazi forces.

With my camera I followed the Allied liberation forces a month after D-Day, exploring a horrific world transformed by war: flattened towns and shattered lives. I wanted to record it all – and that led me to witness terrible things....

But there was joy too: the smiles of children free at last, and adults who knew that Hitler was defeated and peace had come. In 1945 I took photographs of Hitler's Munich apartment, posing in his bathtub with my muddy boots. These were pictures to cheer up the troops and the folks back home.

After the war I suffered from Post Traumatic Stress Disorder (PTSD). My unflinching stare, that explored and recorded Europe's wartime horror, came with a price and I paid it – but showing the world the truth was worth every dime.

Lee photographed the horrors of the liberated Nazi concentration camps at Buchenwald and Dachau, showing historical evidence nobody could deny. Her camera lens made the world witness what human beings could do to one another.

Mary Leakey

1913 - 1996, UK

Archaeologist who explored the history of our human ancestors

Mary Leakey's story

I was born in London but spent much of my childhood in France. My exploring began with a spotted horse....

I was 12 years old when I was taken to see the famous Pech Merle cave, where ancient people had decorated the walls with stencilled hand shapes and animal paintings, including a beautiful spotted horse. It was breathtaking to witness human history stretching back into the distant past and it left me with so many unanswered questions.... Our ancestors must have had ancestors too, perhaps going back to apes? Could there be fossil evidence of this, waiting to be discovered? I wanted to find those answers for myself.

Mary went on to discover more amazing things. Between 1976 and 1981 she uncovered a trail of fossilised footprints where our human ancestors had walked across volcanic ash 3.6 million years ago.

By 1936 I was exploring Africa with my husband, Louis Leakey, excavating likely areas and searching for fossil evidence. By the 1950s our three young sons were helping too, and by 1959 we had found stone tools in Tanzania that were two million years old. This was exciting and we suspected we were on to something big.

Then, one day, I spotted a large fragment of a fossilised skull; next, a chunk of jawbone with two large teeth. Slowly but surely, over the next few weeks we found enough fragments to rebuild the skull and make a replica. We called it *Paranthropus boisei* and because of his huge powerful teeth and jaw the newspapers nicknamed him 'nutcracker man'. And so I began to find my answers under the African sun – and my life's work, exploring the history of the human race.

Barbara Hillary

1931- 2019, USA

First African-American woman to reach
the North and South Poles

Barbara Hillary's story

I was brought up in Harlem, New York. We were very poor and my
widowed mother worked as a cleaner to support me. But there was no
such thing as mental poverty in our home. I loved to read and one of
my favourite books was *Robinson Crusoe*. I worked hard at school and
college and got myself Bachelor's and Master's degrees.

Despite being diagnosed with breast cancer, I followed my career
path and worked for 55 years as a nurse.... I was always active in my
community and was the founder and editor of *The Peninsula Magazine* for
Queens, New York. Later I became a campaigner to raise awareness about
climate change, and though I became very ill with lung cancer I travelled to
Mongolia as part of my awareness campaign.

I was always a bit of a daredevil, and after I retired from nursing I began
dog-sledding in Canada for sport. When I learned that no black woman had
reached the North Pole, I decided to have a go at that! First I had to raise
money and learn to ski, but I did it, I reached the North Pole in 2007! Not only
that but four years later, in 2011, I stood at the South Pole. Not bad going for a
79-year-old.

SOUTH
POLE
I did it! With perseverance, determination and respect for the way my mother raised me.

Two more great explorers…

Dian Fossey (1932-1985, USA) made the mountains of Rwanda her home for nearly 20 years, exploring and studying gorilla behaviour. Her book, *Gorillas in the Mist*, tells the world about the dangers gorillas still face. It made her a lot of enemies among local poachers and corrupt officials.

Biruté Galdikas (born 1946, Lithuania/Canada) was, like Dian Fossey, recruited by Mary and Louis Leakey. She studied orangutans in Borneo and revolutionised human understanding of this threatened species.

Jane Goodall

Born 1934, UK
Trailblazing naturalist and conservationist

Jane Goodall's story

When I was very young, my father gave me a lifesize toy chimpanzee called Jubilee! Family friends were horrified and thought it would give me nightmares, but Jubilee gave me the sweetest dreams. And later those dreams came true....

I was 23 when I visited Africa for the first time. I wanted to see real chimpanzees in the wild and I met Louis and Mary Leakey, who were studying fossils of *hominids*, our ape ancestors. They encouraged me to go to the Gombe Stream Reserve in Tanzania. That was the beginning of 30 years living in the wild, exploring the behaviour of chimpanzees!

At Gombe it took two years before the chimps accepted me as a member of their troop. Now I could study their everyday behaviour. My groundbreaking research showed that wild chimps have personalities, with thoughts and feelings like our own. I gave them names: David Greybeard, Gigi, Frodo.... I was able to prove that chimps make and use tools, and that they are not vegetarians, but omnivores like humans. I watched them hunting as a team to catch and eat smaller colobus monkeys. Chimps are loving and caring; they share food and look after one another... and yet they have a darker side too, waging war and killing rival groups, just as humans do.

In 1977 I set up the Jane Goodall Institute to help conserve and teach about wild primates and all wild animal habitats. Now I spend my time spreading the vital message about the threats to wildlife and our whole environment. *"Every individual counts. Every individual has a role to play. Every individual makes a difference."*

Sylvia Earle's story

I grew up on Florida's beautiful west coast, where my love of nature was able to thrive. I would stare with awe at the rolling ocean, determined one day to discover some of its secrets.

I studied science until, after many years of university education, I received my Ph.D. Then, in 1970, I was selected to lead the all-female team of the Tektite II project. This was the world's first underwater laboratory, 50 feet below the tropical seas of the Caribbean, where we studied marine life at the bottom of the ocean. I made a record-breaking submersion in a deep-sea diving suit, sinking 381 metres (1,250 feet) to the ocean floor near the Virgin Islands.

I was also a founder of Deep Ocean Engineering. We built the *Deep Rover*: a little research submarine that could reach to incredible depths of 1,000 metres (3,300 feet) below the surface.

I have spent my career leading teams to investigate the ocean's health, from the effects of oil pollution to the damage to coral reef habitats. Since 1998 I have been National Geographic's explorer-in-residence, and that year I was also Time magazine's first Hero for the Planet.

In 2009 I founded Mission Blue, a project very close to my heart, to establish protected marine nature reserves where wildlife can thrive and research can be carried out. This is urgent work. Our actions over the next ten years will determine the state of the ocean for the next 1,000 years.

Even now, after a lifetime exploring the world's oceans and learning many of their secrets, I love to stand and gaze with awe at the rolling waves, *'the blue heart of our planet'*.

> The best scientists and explorers ask questions and have a sense of wonder.

Sylvia Earle

Born 1935, USA

Marine Biologist and Oceanographer

Another great explorer...

Rachel Carson (1907-1964, USA) grew up on a farm, learning how plants and animals depend on one another for food in what we call a food chain. Rachel became a great scientist, an explorer of microscopic worlds. Her 1962 book, *Silent Spring,* exposed the dangers of DDT, a pesticide used in farming that was entering food chains and poisoning wildlife and humans.

Valentina Tereshkova

Born 1937, Russia

First Woman in Space

It is I, Seagull! Everything is fine. How beautiful the Earth is... everything is going well.

Valentina Tereshkova's story

Let me tell you how joining a parachute club as a 22-year-old daredevil led me to become the first woman in space!

I was born and brought up in the USSR (now Russia), where I first worked in a textile mill, but my parachute hobby helped me to join the newly formed Soviet Female Cosmonaut Corps. My training was intense and dizzy, but I stuck it out. I wanted to be the first space-woman! And in 1963 I was chosen to fly a solo space mission in *Vostok 6*.

Take-off was noisy and scary as, alone in my tiny capsule, I was blasted into space by a huge rocket. But once I was in space-orbit, everything became calm and peaceful. I took photos and kept a log, orbiting the Earth 48 times. My mission helped scientists to study Earth's atmosphere and the effects of space travel on women.

After almost three days in space I re-entered Earth's atmosphere and ejected as planned, four miles (six kilometres) up. It took four hours for me to float down. When I landed I was greeted as a hero of my motherland, the Soviet Union.

I'm still the only woman to have flown a solo space mission. I went on to become a cosmonaut instructor, training a new generation of space-women. I'm an old lady now… but do you know what I dream of doing one day?
Flying to the planet Mars!

Cameras were placed in the capsule to broadcast live footage on TV. Valentina's call sign was *Seagull*.

Valentina made her first parachute jump in 1959 at the age of 22.

Valentina's cosmonaut training included isolation tests, centrifuge and thermo-chamber tests, decompression chamber testing, and pilot training in jet fighters.

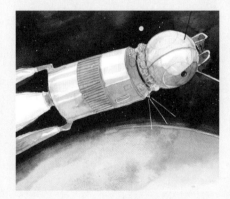

She graduated to pilot Vostok 6, orbiting 48 times around planet Earth.

Junko Tabei

1939 - 2016, Japan

First woman to reach the summit of Mount Everest

Junko Tabei's story

I was born in Japan near Fukushima. I was a frail child but I loved to gaze at our local mountains that seemed somehow to be smiling down at me.

At university I met male students who had a climbing club. I wanted to join, but those boys didn't want to climb with a girl and some even suggested I only wanted to join the club to find a husband. So in 1969 I founded the Ladies Climbing Club – strictly no men allowed! I climbed many mountains with my all-female group before tackling the biggest and scariest of all: Mount Everest.

To save money we made our own gloves from recycled car-seat covers and sewed our own sleeping bags, stuffing them with goose feathers. Then, in 1975, we set off. On the climb, our camp was buried by an avalanche. I was unconscious when they dug me out! But I pressed on and 12 days later, on 16th May, with my Sherpa, Ang Tshering, by my side, I stood on the summit of Everest.

I went on to climb many more high mountains, appearing on TV as the first woman to climb the highest summits on seven continents... But I became more and more aware of the need to look after the mountains. Too many climbers left unwanted equipment and food tins littering the beautiful landscapes. It seemed to me that messy humans were making the mountains sad. So I led 'clean-up' climbs, to help the mountains smile again.

At ten years old I climbed my first mountain with a school group, and longed to do more.

In 2019 a mountain range on the faraway planet Pluto was named in my honour. I hope that one day a future generation of women explorers will climb it.

Mae Jemison

Born 1956, USA

First black woman in space

Mae Jemison's story

I was raised in Chicago and I loved school, especially Maths. At university I graduated with degrees in both Chemical Engineering and African-American Studies. Then I took a medical degree and became a doctor, working as a volunteer with the Peace Corps. But I wanted something else. I wanted to explore space, like my childhood heroes in the TV series *Star Trek*!

So I applied to NASA and in 1987, out of 2,000 applicants, I was one of only 15 people selected. Right away the press called me the 'first black female astronaut'! But I didn't get into space straight away. I spent time on the ground, working with computers and in labs doing technical design.

Then, in 1992, I was chosen for an eight-day space mission on board the space shuttle *Endeavour*. I orbited Earth 127 times and logged over 190 hours in space. Heroes inspire all of us and I carried a photo of Bessie Coleman with me into space.

During my mission I began all my communications with planet Earth by quoting another hero. I would say, 'Hailing frequencies open!' That was the catch-phrase of my favourite *Star Trek* character, Lieutenant Uhura. In my eyes she really was the first black astronaut, even if only on TV. Imagine my excitement when, years later, I guest-starred in *Star Trek* myself!

It's your life.
Go on and do all
you can with it.

Another great explorer...

Kalpana Chawla (USA/India, 1962 - 2003) was born in India but emigrated to the USA when she was 20. She was the first woman of Indian origin to go into space, on the shuttle *Columbia* in 1997, travelling 10.4 million miles (16.7 million kilometres) during 252 orbits of the Earth. She was tragically killed in 2003, with all crew, when their shuttle disintegrated on re-entry to Earth's atmosphere. An asteroid was named in her memory.

Arunima Sinha

Born 1988, India

First female amputee to climb Mount Everest and Mount Vinson

Arunima Sinha's story

Growing up in Uttar Pradesh, India, I loved sport and was selected for the National Volleyball team. I was a strong, independent woman and I wanted to stand up for justice. My ambition was to join the CISF, the Central Armed Police Force. And that's when my life changed….

I was invited to attend an exam for the special police force in Delhi. But when I boarded the train I was attacked by robbers, who tried to steal my bag and gold chain. In the struggle I was pushed out of the speeding train. Surgeons had to amputate my left leg to save my life. I had also fractured my spine and needed metal pins in my other leg. But I fought for my life and, learning to walk with an artificial limb, I was already planning to do something big.

I decided to climb the highest mountains in the world, starting with Mount Everest! I began to train until, after over a year of pain and gain, I was ready…. My climbing buddy was Susan Mahout, a US Air Force instructor. After 52 days, on 21 May, 2013, we stood together on the summit. As I hoisted Mother India's flag, I gave thanks to the Almighty who had helped me stay strong.

I carried on fighting, by climbing the highest mountains on seven continents. In 2014 I wrote a book, *Born Again on the Mountain*, and in 2015 I received India's Padma Shri award for my courage. In 2019 I became the first female amputee to climb the highest peak in Antarctica, Mount Vinson. Now I give talks to inspire and motivate people: if I can fight back from a life-changing tragedy, then you can too!

Another great explorer...

Namira Salim (born 1975, Pakistan) is the first Pakistani person to reach the North and South Poles, the first Asian to skydive over Mount Everest, and the first Pakistani woman to travel into space.

Set your goals high in life and don't stop until you reach there.

Glossary

American Civil War – the war to abolish slavery, fought from 1861 to 1865, by the Union states against the Confederate states of the south, who still supported slavery.

Astronomer – a scientist who studies the stars.

Biologist – a scientist who studies living things.

Bloomers – a form of trousers for women, made popular by Amelia Bloomer (1818-1894).

Comet – an icy rock that, when close to the sun, warms and begins to release gases. This makes the 'tail' of the comet.

Concentration camp – a prison intended to hold people who have not committed any crime but whom a government has deprived of human rights because of their race or opinions.

Conservationist – someone who acts to protect or preserve the natural world.

Crimean War – a war fought from 1853 to 1856 between Russia and an alliance made up of France, United Kingdom, Sardinia and the Ottoman Empire (land ruled by Turkey).

Dwarf elliptical galaxy – a galaxy whose shape is a flattened circle and which may contain a billion or more stars (small to astronomers).

Ketch – a two-masted sailing boat.

Medieval – the time between about 600 and 1400 CE.

Middle East – a region that includes parts of Western Asia, all of Egypt and Turkey.

Milky Way – the galaxy that contains our Solar System and up to 400 billion other stars.

Naturalist – someone who studies plants and animals living in the natural world.

Poachers – people who kill wild animals illegally for food or profit.

Nazis – A political party and huge military power that arose in Germany in the 1930s, led by Adolf Hitler.

Omnivore – an eater of both meat and plants.

Post Traumatic Stress Disorder – mental health issues that may develop after experiences of war or other shocking events.

Paranthropus boisei – a scientific name. Paranthropus means 'alongside human' and boisei is in honour of Charles Boise, who sponsored the Leakeys' work.

Pseudonym – a false name.

Royal Geographical Society – the United Kingdom's professional body for geography, founded in 1830.

Sami – indigenous peoples, sometimes called Lapps, who live in Lapland, an area that straddles parts of Sweden, Norway, Finland and Russia.

Shoshone nation – one of the many nations of indigenous peoples of the Americas.

Star Trek – an American science fiction series that began in 1966 and was famous for its diversity.

The Allies – the countries that united to fight and defeat Germany and her own allies during the Second World War.

The Peace Corps – an independent US organisation of volunteers that helps poor and developing countries.

Typhus – an infectious disease spread by lice, fleas or mites.

Vikings – warriors from Scandinavia who conquered and settled parts of Scotland, Ireland, England and parts of Europe as well as Iceland and Greenland.